Parenting Within

&

A Lifetime Mentor

Two Different Programs
With One Goal and One Purpose

A Better Future Will Always Lead To

A Better Tomorrow

Parenting Within

By: Peggie Wright

Introduction

As a child, there are natural expectations you have of your parents. From the time a child is conceived in the womb, they could feel the love of their mother. This love grows as the unborn child is receiving all the nurturing, nutrients, caring, and even conversations the mother (parents) transfer to the child. It is said that the child expresses their joy and happiness through the movement in their mother's womb. (nypost.com, 10/23/2016). Fast forwarding, nine months later, this conception is fully developed and ready for delivery into a world that you have already prepared them for through your nurturing, caring, nutrients (feedings), and communication. Yet, the baby's expectations and what's required of you are different and more demanding.

Several Psychosocial theorists support the importance of nurturing as a foundation for producing and raising healthy children; hence. referencing Erik Erikson's theory *'trust vs. mistrust'*, which is the beginning of a healthy esteem for the child. According to Erikson, from birth to twelve months, the infant must learn that adults can be trusted; not just adults, but their parents. What does this trust look like – when I cry you hear me and figure out what my needs are; am I hungry, do I need my diaper changed, do I need a bath, or do I just need your assuring smiles and hugs along with me feeling the security of laying across your check while getting my back rubbed? Adversely, mistrust could look like anxiety, fear, and an unpredictable world where their needs are not met. Henceforth, this basic psychosocial development could most likely produce adolescents/grown-ups who are trustworthy and sees the world as a safe place or grows up with a sense of mistrust for people and not sure of themselves. I came from a single-family home where I was the second oldest of eight (4boys/4girls). As a teenage mom my mother struggled to provide for us – food, clothing, housing – yet she did it. However, it was even more difficult for my mother to parent us. There's a saying that "anybody can make a baby, but everybody is not fit for a mother or know how to be a parent". So, it led me to define the two.

According to Webster's dictionary, a mother is a female parent who produces; gives birth to a child. But parenting is defined as caring for the child, raising, rearing, upbringing, fathering, motherhood; hence, the process of taking care of children until they are old enough to take care of themselves, and, to bring forth and raise to maturity through care and education. Personally speaking, I was not raised by my mother, nor was I cared for until I was able to take care of myself. Nevertheless, I was raised, but by a community of people. Therefore, I have a personal stake in knowing and identifying with children who are nurturing deficient.

STATISTICS / RESEARCH

- 1960 ± 95% of babies born into married households

- Currently

- ± 64% of children living with 2 parents who are married

- ± 26% are single parent

- ± 15% are remarried

- ± 7% are cohabitating

40 FACTS ABOUT TWO PARENT FAMILIES

https://gillespieshields.com/40-facts-two-parent-families/

BENEFITS OF A TWO PARENT/MARRIED HOUSEHOLD

- The child has a solid intact family structure

- Positive impact on a child's present and future wellbeing

- Child is less likely to experience academic, social, emotional, and cognitive problems

- The child has access to more economic and community resources; parents' time, money, and energy are tied together

- Influenced on reducing out of wedlock births, increase high school and college graduation rates

- The child has a greater potential of gaining high employment rates

- Fathers spend more family time

- The child has a higher level of achievement and less likely to have behavior issues

- Children probability of living in poverty is reduced by about 82%

- Ginther & Pollack; Manning & Lamb; Amato, Howard & Reeves

FACTS ABOUT
TWO PARENT FAMILIES
DIVORCE / ENVIRONMENTAL TURMOIL

• Children are more likely to develop health problems following a divorce

• Headaches, injury, speech defects

• Are more likely to be abused and neglected

• Children of stepfathers are more likely to be suspended

• Expelled from school and engage in delinquent behavior

• Problems getting along with teachers

• Has low-grade point average

• Environmental turmoil/married couples/cohabitation

• Instability

• Constant changing of schools

• Constant changes in employment

NOTE: children who experience divorce, separation, or death do not perform well or achieve academically. (Nyarko 2007)

SOCIOCULTURAL IMPACT ON DEVELOPMENT

LEV VYGOTSKY

• According to Vygotsky adults are an important source of cognitive development and place considerably more emphasis on social factors contributing to cognitive development.

• Adults transmit their culture's tools of intellectual adaptation that children internalize.

• Vygotsky states cognitive development stems from social interactions from guided learning within the zone of proximal development as children and their partner's co-construct knowledge.

• For Vygotsky, the environment in which children grow up will influence how they think and what they think about.

• Suggest a child's social world defines their thinking; learning is best supported at opportune times when the caregiver aids their learning

NOTE: It's asserted that the absence of the missing parent to guide, discipline, direct, model, and teach may be one of the causes that a child from a single-parent family may not perform academically at their full potential. (Rothstein, 2004)

PARENTING WITHIN MENTORING PROGRAM PROPOSAL

Based on the information presented, I would like to propose to you the "Parenting Within Mentoring Program" (PWMP).

• Purpose: the purpose of the Parenting Within Mentoring Program is to provide parental guidance, support, encouragement, motivation, and nurturing to students who show signs of being malnourished in these areas. The PWMP will serve to bridge the gap between parents and their child(ren).

• Statistics have shown that single parents (mothers and fathers), children of divorced parents, stepfathers, and adults who cohabitate could have a significant effect on a child's lack of academic success.

• It was asserted that "when children raised in a single-parent household are left alone for long periods or left in the hands of uninvolved caregivers, their academic skills are not being fully supported". (Knox & Virginia, 1996)

• It was also asserted that "the absence of the missing parent to guide, discipline, direct, model, and teach may be one of the causes that a child may not perform at their full potential. (Rothstein, 2004).

GOALS/ Services Provided

Goals:

- To build confidence in the student

- To help the student identify their strengths and build on them; thus, will also strengthen their weaknesses

- To bridge the gaps in academic and parental guidance

- To improve communication and personal skills of students and parents

- Reinforce study skills and knowledge of subjects

- Develop leadership and decision making

Services:

- Time management

- Conflict resolution

- Communication skills

- Priority setting

ROLE PLAYERS / CRITERIA

Role Players:

- The program is open to recruiting educators, parents, community activists, college students (21 and over for elementary; 25 and over for middle school; and 30 and over for high school), business professionals, and retirees.

Criteria:

- First and foremost, the mentor MUST respect the wishes of the parent concerning their child
- The mentor must be willing to work with a diversity of students
- The mentor must be able to commit to a minimum of 3 months; with 2-3 visits per week

- The mentor must be objective and fair
- The mentor must be compassionate and genuine
- The mentor must be approachable, reliable, available, and a good listener

- The mentor must NOT be judgmental or bias
- The mentor must be willing to share what they know

- The mentor must have a general knowledge of education; especially in the area of literacy and math

- The mentor must develop trust and respect with the students and parents

- The mentor must show students that they care

The **Parenting Within Program** is designed to support the families, schools, and the community; with the hope of collaboratively diminishing and/or eliminating some of the current barriers seen in the education field. Barriers such as low attendance, poor academic grades, discipline referrals and other behaviors that may be contributing to the child's lack of achievement.

My heart's desire is to help students and families bridge the gap of deficiency for the betterment of our children's future. Thank you for taking the time to read and consider this program.

Peggie Wright

A Lifetime Mentor

By: Shakiri Hooper

Not a Perfect World

But a Better Outcome

Introduction

The love and care that I have for children began in my home with my own. Having children was truly a blessing. My children pushed me to want more for myself. I wanted to protect my children, guide, nurture and encourage them to do great things in life. I was raised in a single-family home with my three sisters. Our mother did the best she could for us. Important solid foundation such as structure were lacking in our lives. Confusion and doubt were a part of my life leaving me unsure of the path and future I wanted. I was struggling with reading, math, and major issues at home. When I made it to high school, there was so much peer pressure. I began to skip school. I would often cry because I wanted a better life, but I did not know how to get it. One teacher stopped me at the gate of Kashmere High School right before I was planning to skip and walk off campus yet again. He told me to get back in the school, he encouraged me and said I could do so much more. This may be hard to believe but, I walked back in the school with an angry look on my face, fusing and making gestures that gave him the impression to mind his own business, but inside, I was so relieved, thankful and desperate for someone to just stop me before I jumped off that cliff.

That music teacher retired and eventually after failing 9th and 10th grade and watching my supposed to be class graduate, I dropped out of school. Soon, I met a person that helped me enroll in a GED program at Kashmere High School about six months later. I was teased by the other students in class because my practice test scores were the lowest in class. My teacher, family and a group of others encouraged me to push through. February 28, 1996, I was issued a Texas Certificate of High School Equivalency, my GED. Today, I devoted myself, starting with my own children, to help, lead, guide, direct and pull children up in hopes they will not jump off the cliff.

Personal Thoughts

This deep heartfelt desire to help other children grew even stronger when I started working with children. I have worked in many daycares, private schools, Houston ISD and Cyfair ISD school district. I have been with the school district for over 12 years. I have seen firsthand how mentoring makes a big difference in children's lives. No, I was not a teacher nor was I an administrator. I was a clerk that had the opportunity to work with, lead, encourage, and build up so many children. My first opportunity to become a mentor was at the Contemporary Learning Center in Houston Independent School District. The desire to help children did not stop there. At Garden Oaks Montessori Magnet, myself along with my colleagues designed an after-school program called Junior Ambassadors. We taught children the word of God on their level. Children spoke up about being bullied, supporting their families, and making wise decisions. Parents gave us testimonies about how their children's attitudes changed at school and home. Every individual on this planet needs to be encouraged. The power of motivation is so strong, that it can lead a person to do horrific things in life or push them to greatness. Motivation can be given to build or tear down. If you are not motivated by the right person or for the right purpose you may go down the wrong path. Let us build a system that will give kids the push they need!

Lowering the Dropout Rate

Many students make it to high school and drop out. You see students with more stress, anxiety, and higher peer pressure. That small important group that gets lost in the system because they are from a low-income family, has behavioral issues, or is labeled and has an IEP, already has low expectations from some teachers and even administrators in the school. I have seen Assistant Principals in elementary and high school look at the work or behavior of the student and make the statement "Oh they have a learning disability", and that child is not seen as nothing more than a statistic. If or when that child makes it to high school, they may have a low IQ because they were ignored or not expected to do better from elementary to middle school. If these students manage to graduate high school, college is normally not in their future. I heard an elementary teacher with her own words make a statement about a student, she stated: ***"She will probably make a good store stocker"***. In a time with a pandemic, we see that store stockers are important and needed. This teacher did not make this statement with the idea that a store stocker was an important role in life but assured this student would be limited because she was not as smart as the other students in the class. We can work together and lower the dropout rate, assure that every child regardless of race or gender is offered a trade after high school, monitor and guide those who are considered to have a higher rate of being a part of the prison pipeline, support students on their journey and give hope to those who have never seen hope.

School Districts

The school district is made up of several units, positions, and departments. We have cafeteria staff, custodians, counselors, department chairs, teacher assistants, and secretaries just to name a few. When we hear school, the first position many of us may think of is a teacher. A teacher is a person who instructs, educates, and or trains our children in the school. They prepare them for a test, teach them skills that will better their education and understanding. Teachers also can be the voice of reason and a mediator to help solve conflicts among students. Another position that may come to your mind when you hear school is principal. The principal is a person who oversees the school. A principal has a tremendous responsibility. I have had the opportunity to meet and work under many amazing principals. Principals are placed in positions to sustain the well-being of the schools' success. I have seen principals pick up trash, teach the children, load books on carts, and even pass out food trays. A school can become a family type of setting. On average, a school-age child spends 7.17 hours a day in school and about 180 days on an average, (nces.ed.gov). These numbers exclude, after school programs, tutoring, football practice, and other programs designed at the school. On a regular school day, children spend more time in school than with their families. Each school district needs to ask this question, "Is the time being utilized appropriately?" In elementary, I have seen teachers spending two hours trying to convivence a student to come in the class. I have seen students roam the halls in middle and high school. Many students have already been decided and placed in a category by teachers and staff as a lost cause. Stress and overwhelming situations are not healthy for the staff nor students. Every person at the school has a purpose, but no one person can do it all. The principals, janitors, clerks, superintendent, and hundreds of others are important and a crucial factor for the success of that district. A district's priority is the children. A successful and productive school can bring about successful productive students. Rather in the area of behavior, grades, or artistic ability, children hold the key to a healthy future. Mentoring is absolute in maintaining the success and stability of our youth. I love the fact that volunteers sacrifice their time to help others. This is a sacrifice that I have made all too often. I do not regret any of the programs, meetings, nor groups I was a part of with my own children, but it was a sacrifice. I am thankful to see the students I was able to guide be successful in life. That music teacher that took me back in the school was one in a million. He had his students to deal with but took the time to stop me from making another mistake. I never had the chance to say thank you. A teacher can put on a role as a counselor and a counselor can put on the role of a teacher. The principals I worked with that picked up the trash alongside the custodians still carried the title as a principal. They understand that the school district has many members just like a family that support each other. The program I am proposing allows Mentors to be paid staff personnel. Volunteer Mentors are always needed in the school and that will never stop, with or without this program. My son is a student who has benefited from the volunteers at the local church near his school. He does not see the person often, nor is there any consistency. The volunteers have a life outside of their volunteer hours. Allowing a group of mentors to be paid staff will benefit parents, students, and teachers.

Inspiration to Create This Program

While working in Montessori, I saw a different system in place than what I saw as a child or even in other schools I have worked in. The grade levels at the Montessori school were Pre-Kinder to 8th grade. Students were in Pre-k and Kindergarten together until they went to the 1st grade. All the classes had two or more grade levels. The teachers at the Montessori school either had 1st – 3rd-grade students, 4th – 6th-grade students, or 7th – 8th-grade students in their classes. The teachers taught all the core subjects. While working at the school, I notice a connection that many students had with their teachers and classmates. Many of those students were in the same class and grade level until 8th grade. This stability made their relationships and friendships even stronger. Most of the students loved their teachers and looked forward to seeing them for the next three years. There were positive outcomes for the students being taught by the same teacher for two to three years. Teachers were able to give information about the student to parents, counselors, social workers, and administration. They knew the students and developed a relationship with them for the past 2-3 years, therefore, the teachers were able to identify any concerning changes the student had. The lack of social skills was extremely low. The students were in a classroom with different grade levels and that gave them a role similar to an older sibling or a younger sibling needing help. Teachers often assigned older students as mentors. Another benefit to the Montessori system is the advanced learning that often took place. Younger students were curious to learn because they saw others learning. They watched the other students work on table or floor work and they became anxious to learn. I loved the program, but the system is not for every student. Some changes also needed to be made on the child's behalf. All children are different. Their personalities can be challenging for some teachers. In Montessori school, there were times that the teacher and students' personalities were not in sync with each other. Students were moved from one classroom to the other. Sometimes students were allowed to sit in other classrooms for the morning or afternoon to evaluate that student's reaction to being in a different class. If the anticipation is that the child will be with the teacher for 2-3 years, there should be a healthy fit for the student. That is why the school does everything in its power and uses all its available resources to assure that the students are getting the best education and a teacher that will support their child's learning experience.

Montessori has positive benefits that will support the Lifetime Mentors program.

A Lifetime Mentor Proposal

I am suggesting for the school district to hire and incorporate a paid mentoring staff department. A group of dedicated mentors who want to build a relationship with the students. This amazing group of individuals will be **Lifetime Mentors**.

What is A Lifetime Mentor?

Lifetime Mentors are not mentors that meet with the students once a week or for half a school year and the students are never seen again. Lifetime Mentors are a group that is committed to the students for the end of their school term. They will be paid, contracted personnel. This group will be assigned, but not limited to keeping track of the child's social skills, behavior, conduct, and overall progress in school. They are not here to take the place of other mentoring groups, nor counselors. Lifetime Mentors goal is to mentor, support, and guide.

Benefits of A Paid Staff Mentoring Program

- Students and the parents will build a relationship with the mentor

- The student will see their mentor four times a week

- The mentor will be a staff member of the district which allows easy access, close monitoring, and healthy communication

- The mentor will be with them every step of their school year

- The mentor will be well trained from the district

- The mentor will become familiar with the school setting and procedures

- Paid staff mentors can orchestrate/schedule the volunteer mentors from the community.

Goal

Our goal is to change statistics. If we work together as a community, we will have higher graduation numbers and fewer dropouts. My time working as a high school secretary has allowed me to see firsthand the need for intervention in the schools. The Civil Rights Project facilitates the use of data by those preparing for or engaged in, meaningful actions to replace harsh and ineffective disciplinary policies and practices with approaches that are effective for children, schools, and their communities, (civil rights project). Their goal is designed to break the prison pipeline. This project document excessive disciplinary exclusion increases awareness, enhance the capacity of advocates, support community groups and school districts, and serve as a watchdog function with data and analyzing federal and state policy, (civil rights project). Lifetime Mentors will work with many organizations such as this that aligns with the goals of the school district. This position will not take the place of those teachers and staff that love to be a shoulder for the children to cry on. Remember we are all working together. Every person in the life of these children should be here to help pick up the pieces with hopes of a better future.

Positive Effects

- Build a support team with parents, students, staff, and community

- Lower discipline issues in all grade levels

- Minimize the number of students effected by the prison pipeline system

- Higher graduation rates

- Encourage furthering education past high school

- Assure that documentation is accurate and complete

How will the program work?

I love this program because there is consistency involved. In the example chart below, you will see mentors 1,2, and 3. Mentor One will have his or her students from 3rd to 5th grade. During 5th grade year, child A, B, and C will meet their middle school Lifetime Mentor along with a parent/guardian and counselor. With high anticipation of graduation from middle school child A, B, and C will meet their High School Mentor along with a parent/guardian and counselor. Each mentor will keep a record of the students' progress and that information is passed forward to each mentor. Please see an example chart on the following page.

Example Chart

Elementary Mentor One 3rd – 5th	Middle School Mentor Two 6th – 8th	High School Mentor Three 9th – 12th
Child A	Child A	Child A
Child B	Child B	Child B
Child C	Child C	Child C

The chart shows balance and consistency in the life of the student with their assigned mentor. Each student apart of the program will have stability and consistency. This chart reveals the program working in the perfect world. If a child continues in the school district, they will have the same mentor and be a part of the same program until graduation.

Pros to The Program

- Students and the parents will build a relationship with the mentor

- The student will see their mentor four times a week

- The mentor will be a staff member of the district which allows easy access, and healthy communication

- This mentor will be with them every step of their school year

- You do not have to look for mentors or get a sign-up sheet

- Students will know their mentors prior to going to middle or high school

- Principals, counselors, and administration can utilize the mentors at the school's campuses

- Students will have a chance to meet other students apart of the program

Cons to The Program

- Assuring the student have a good fit

- Students leave the district

- Assigning mentors in the middle of the school year

- Mentors that do not have a heart to service the students

Addressing the Cons

o Assuring the student have a good fit

This is not an easy task. Mentors should work as a team to assure the child is receiving the motivation they need. If the program is not a good fit for the student, the parents and school will be notified. This process will not take place until all resources has been utilized.

o   Students leave the district

We hope that the student stays with the school district until graduation. If this is not the case, we will give the student a good luck ceremony and a certificate in remembrance of being a part of the program. We want the students to be successful in any school district they choose to be a part of.

o   Assigning mentors in the middle of the school year

This may be challenging depending on the student and the grade level; however, with the help of teachers, counselors, and administration, we will work together to make the transition a success.

o   Mentors that do not have a heart to service the students

If there are any mentors who are not providing the best support and care, they will be reported to the Mentoring Department head.

Common Questions and Answers

Which students are eligible to have a Lifetime Mentor?

Lifetime Mentors will work with students in Elementary, Middle, and High School. Children who are at risk or dealing with behavior issues will qualify for a mentor. However, these are not the only criteria that will qualify a student to have a mentor. Parents, principals' counselors, and teachers will have the opportunity to recommend a child to be a part of the program.

What makes this program different?

Schools, churches, and outreach programs see the need for mentors. They recruit volunteers every year in hopes of bringing in more individuals to be a guide for children. The need is evident. This is a program that has the same desires, except this is a paid staff. There will not be a need to recruit volunteers. Lifetime mentors will be there at the beginning of the school year just like other staff members that want to support the students.

How many mentors will be provided for each school?

In order for this program to be fully supported, there will need to be available funds. The number of mentors will depend on the budget for that school district. Mentors will work Monday thru Thursday at their assigned schools and groups. Fridays will allow the mentors to summit data, analysis, and suggestions for the school district personnel to review.

Will a student have the opportunity to enroll in the middle of his/her high school year?

Students are not limited to starting in the 3rd grade; however, it is crucial to build a relationship at an early age. If a student does not receive their fundamentals in math or reading in elementary it could affect the child in other grades. Causing them to have a hard time in middle school and most likely high school. This does not suggest the student cannot learn, however, there will be evidence of deficiency in their learning skills. This is the same understanding we should have with building a relationship with the students. We must start in elementary if we want the program to be successful.

Will this program do away with volunteers from the community?

Lifetime mentors are designed to bring the community together. They will work with the volunteers in the community as well as the students and staff. The volunteers will also be assigned students. They will work with those students who are not a part of the Lifetime Mentoring program. There will always be a need for volunteers. We cannot build a community without the support of the community.

Are mentors allowed to meet with or pick-up students on the weekend?

Mentors are not allowed to pick up nor drop off students. Lifetime Mentors will follow the same guidelines as any other staff member or volunteer at the school district.

How will students be assigned to mentors?

Prior to enrollment, parents will fill out a form about their child's personality. In hopes that the child will begin in 3rd grade, we will then monitor the student and our mentors to prepare the best fit for the student mentally and emotionally for their elementary, middle school and high school year.

What credentials will the mentors need?

A teacher can have the ability to teach before they ever receive their certification. I am a mentor, teacher, and parent currently without a degree. A Lifetime mentor staff should have experience, 60 college hours or a bachelor's degree. Every Mentor will be trained by the district.

Will special need students be a part of the program?

The program will not discriminate against any children regardless of race, or gender. Students who are special needs will need to be assigned a certified special needs staff mentor that has the experience and a degree in special education.

Thank You

Thank you for taking the time to read this proposal. I am sure that many others want to contribute to change in the world. That change starts with the children. A healthier environment, fewer prisons being built, less crime, higher education, more businesses, growing and stable families, the list can go on and on. In order to see this change, the system has to make adjustments. The school district needs a program with this style and structure. In today's society, children need to have as much support as possible. I have seen the need for more disciplinarians in school from elementary to high school. Schools will bring in more police officers to high schools, AP secretaries to submit the data from students who have behavioral issues, and volunteers who cannot bring stability, but they should also take the time to bring balance, consistency, and hope to those who need it the most. I hope that you please look over this proposal and consider this program to be a part of the school system.

Shakiri R. Hooper

My Hopes

I am hopeful that this program will not be overlooked. I ask that you look at the program from the heart of a mother, wife and a person who love children. I recently received my bachelor's degree in Social Science with and Emphasis in Social Work, November 2020. I did not want to only mentor, but I wanted to be an example. My hope is to help many schools with programs that are geared towards supporting children to be successful in life.

Acknowledgments

I am thankful to God, my family, and friends.

"We are called **Lifetime Mentors** because the experience the child receives will last a Lifetime"

References

https://nces.ed.gov/surveys/sass/tables/sass0708_035_s1s.asp

https://civilrightsproject.ucla.edu/resources/projects/center-for-civil-rights-remedies/school-to-prison-folder

* 9 7 9 8 7 1 3 1 1 9 0 5 8 *